Copyrighted by
Maxfield Parrish 1909.

MAGICIANS
&ENCHANTERS

ELIZABETH RATISSEAU

LAUGHING ELEPHANT   MM11

ISBN 1-883211-48-4

LAUGHING ELEPHANT

3645 INTERLAKE AVENUE NORTH
SEATTLE WASHINGTON 98103

Among the Ancients, who dealt so largely with physical sciences, there seems to have been a common language which could be used to explain the invisible world and its inhabitants; but we of this age have not yet developed such a language.

WALTER YEELING EVANS-WENTZ

Seek not, Oh twice-blessed One, to attain the spiritual essence before the mind absorbs. Not thus is wisdom sought. Only he who hath the mind in leash, and seeth the world as in a mirror can be safely trusted with the inner senses. Only he who knoweth the five senses to be illusion, and that naught remaineth save the two ahead, can be admitted into the secret of the Cruciform transposed.

ANCIENT SCRIPTURE

A magician has been long in the making – his "art" requires untold years of study, a tenacious will, extreme self-discipline, and withdrawal from the usual pleasures of living. Many of the gifts given: divination, prophecy, metamorphosis, control of events, people or animals, cause the magician to be regarded with fear, suspicion and even hatred. The power attached is envied and sought after by others – sometimes to his disappearance, but he returns when needed.

ELIZABETH RATISSEAU

MAGICIANS & ENCHANTERS

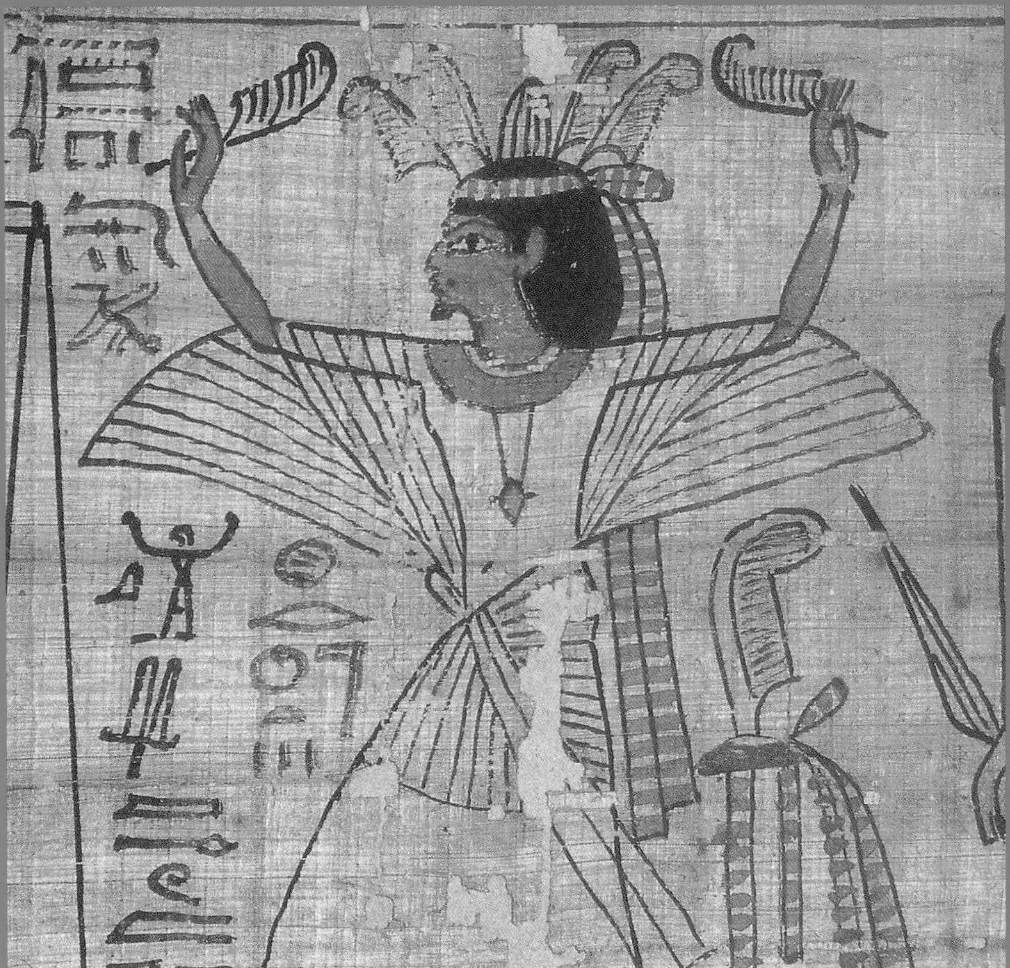

Say: 'I take refuge with the Lord of the Daybreak from the evil of what he has created, from the evil of darkness when it gathers, from the evil of the women who blow on knots, from the evil of an envier when he envies.'

KORAN (CXIII)

No man ever obtained such absolute power over the Jinn as Suleyman. [10th century B.C.] This he did by virtue of a most wonderful talisman...a seal-ring, upon which was engraved "the most great name" of God; and was partly composed of brass, and partly of iron. With the brass he stamped his written commands to the good Jinn; with the iron [which they greatly dread], those to the evil Jinn, or Devils. Over both orders he had unlimited power; as well over the birds and the winds, and, as is generally said, the wild beasts.

PADRAIC COLUM

they follow what the Satans recited over Solomon's kingdom. Solomon disbelieved not,
but the Satans disbelieved, teaching the people sorcery.

KORAN (II, 96)

The recognition by Islam of the existence of Jinn furnished a basis for the belief in magic, to which, however, the attitude of the educated and of serious writers is about the same in most countries; it is not ordinarily recognized as an agent in the course of events, yet may well be admitted into tales of wonder and delight, whereas the superstitious may resort to it for a variety of needs.

D.S. MARGOLIOUTH

There is a curtain, thin as gossamer, clear as glass, strong as iron, that hangs forever between the world of magic and the world that seems to us to be real. And when once people have found one of the little dark spots in that curtain which are marked by magic rings and amulets, and the like, almost anything may happen.

NOEL STREATFIELD ON E. NESBIT

There has never been a society without some concept of the supernatural, some awareness of forces moving in the shadows beyond human understanding.

ANDRÉ AND LYNETTE SINGER

There were, after all, practicing sorcerers, alchemists and treasure hunters in medieval Baghdad and Cairo. Geomancers were consulted regarding business trips and the outcome of sporting events. The powers of magic and the Jinn were not to be doubted.

ROBERT IRWIN

[A] curious, abnormal, not quite human type—Circe dwells far away in the mystic and traceless seas. Cruel, but no more consciously cruel than the child...[her] special power is metamorphosis, [Circe] amuses herself with enticing such wandering mariners as come within her reach to drink magic potions which straightway turn them into swine. Like any other queen of the mermaids, Circe is unmoral rather than immoral.

KIRBY FLOWER SMITH

In song and story, in the long annals of magic itself, there never has been a sorceress to compare with Medea...Medea...is still the archenchantress of all the Occident...She can restore youth, bestow invulnerability, lull the dragon of the golden fleece to slumber, quiet the storms, make the rivers pause in their courses, call down the moon from heaven...But Medea is also beneficent...She heals the wounds of the Argonauts, cures Heracles of his madness, frees the Corinthians from a famine, and is even a prophetess.

KIRBY FLOWER SMITH

These are geometrical designs representing the mysteries of deity and creation, therefore supposed to be of special virtue in rites of evocation and conjuration. Major diagrams are the Triangle; the Double Triangle, forming a six-pointed star and known as the Sign or Seal of Solomon; the Tetragram, a four-pointed star formed by the interlacement of two pillars; and the pentagram, a five pointed star. These signs were traces on paper or parchment or engraved on metals and glass and consecrated to their various uses by special rites.

FROM *THE ENCYCLOPEDIA OF OCCULTISM & ARAPSYCHOLOGY*

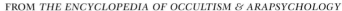

The Pentagram, which in Gnostic schools is called the Blazing Star...is the Star of the Magi...Now if Magic be a reality, if occult science be really the true law of the three worlds, this absolute sign, this sign ancient as history and more ancient, should and does exercise an incalculable influence upon spirits set free from their material envelope.

WADE BASKIN

A TREATISE ON WHITE MAGIC: RULE FOUR

Sound, light, vibration, and the form blend and merge, and thus the work is one. It proceedeth under the law, and naught can hinder now the work from going forward. The man breathes deeply. He concentrates his forces, and drives the thought from him. The Creative Work of Sound. The Science of the Breath.

ALICE A. BAILEY

The Great Magician appears at a time of crisis, in order to introduce the element of positive change. His role is not always recognized since he has many names. As Gandalf the Grey he helped in the far times of Middle Earth to defeat the dark lord.

With Dwarf and Hobbit, Elves and Men,
with mortal and immortal folk
with bird on bough and beast in dens,
in their own secret tongues he spoke

J.R.R. TOLKIEN

With the name Merlin he was present to guide Arthur to his throne...

Merlin came straightway to the king, even as he was bidden...[The King] was ever about him with prayers and entreaties that he would show him somewhat of things that were yet to come,..."Sire," replied Merlin, "this I may not do. I dare not open my lips...save only when needs speak. Should my tongue be unloosed by greed or lightness, should I be puffed up by vanity, then my familiar spirit—that being by whom I know that which I know—would withdraw his inspiration from my breath. My knowledge would depart from me...Let the future take care of itself."

WACE

Merlin in more modern times says...

Light! It is all light. The light is all, and in the light there is only one thing—eternal life. I cannot be created or destroyed. The wizard is not afraid to walk in darkness—indeed he must—because that is where illusion dies.

DEEPAK CHOPRA

A TREATISE ON WHITE MAGIC

The white magician works from the soul level out into the manifested world and seeks to carry out the divine plan, whilst the black magician works from the level of the intellect as he seeks to achieve his own separative ends. The difference is not only that of motive, but also of alignment and the radius of the consciousness and its field of expansion...Only the tested and the true, only the unselfish and the pure can be given the full instructions. It should be borne in mind that the

soul of matter, the anima mundi, is the sentient factor in substance itself. It is the responsiveness of matter throughout the universe and that innate faculty in all forms, from the atom of the physicist, to the solar system of the astronomer, which produces the undeniable intelligent activity which all demonstrate.

ALICE A. BAILEY

It is difficult to estimate the enormous popularity that magic experienced, whether for good or evil, during the Middle Ages. . . . the power it seems to have conferred upon the practitioner was coveted by scores of people

THE ENCYCLOPEDIA OF OCCULTISM
& PARAPSYCHOLOGY

The charms used by medieval witches incorporated prayers and invocations of the Church, in both Latin and Hebrew, as well as more unconventional elements. Use was made of the mystic power of language, magical incantations, being combined with texts already imbued with the potency of the Church. . . . The combination of reasonably sophisticated herbalism and the enactment of a ritual clearly worked, and most members of the community took advantage of the skills that were offered. . . . These practitioners, both men and women, were known by the name "Witch." . . . They were essentially working magicians, although they were paid only small amounts. The local population viewed them as positive, indeed indispensable, but there was always the suspicion that they could turn their skills in more dangerous directions. Popular wisdom tended to endorse the view that all magic has a dark side.

The typically ambivalent attitude towards the wise woman model of a witch [was of] a solitary yet powerful outcast, regarded with both fear and fascination.

ANDRÉ AND LYNETTE SINGER

Two great names in the history of European magic are those of Paracelsus and Agrippa, who outlined the science of medieval magic. They were also the greatest practical magicians of the Middle ages—apart from pure mystics, alchemists, and others—and their thaumaturgic and necromantic experiences were probably never surpassed.

THE ENCYCLOPEDIA OF OCCULTISM & PARAPSYCHOLOGY

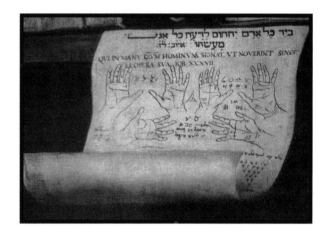

Magic, therefore, combines in a single science that which is most certain in philosophy which is eternal and infallible in religion. It reconciles perfectly and incontestably those two terms so opposed on the first view—faith and reason, science and belief, authority and liberty. It furnishes the human mind with an instrument of philosophical and religious certainty as exact as mathematics, and even accounting for the infallibility of mathematics themselves. . . . There is an incontestable truth; there is an infallible method of knowing that truth; while those who attain this knowledge and adopt it as a rule of life, can endow their life with a sovereign power which can make them masters of all inferior things, all wandering spirits, or, in other words, arbiters and kings of the world.

ELIPHAS LEVI

"The magical is a great hidden wisdom, and reason is a great open folly. No armour shields against magic for it strikes at the inward spirit of life. Of this we may rest assured, that through full and powerful imagination only can we bring the spirit of any man into an image. No conjuration, no rites are needful; circle-making and the scattering of incense are mere humbug and jugglery. the human spirit is so great a thing that no man can express it; eternal and unchangeable as God Himself is the mind of man' and could we rightly comprehend the mind of man, nothing would be impossible to us upon the earth. Through faith the imagination is invigorated and completed, for it really happens that every doubt mars its perfection. Faith must strengthen imagination, for faith establishes the will. Because man did not perfectly believe and imagine, the result is that arts are uncertain when they might be wholly certain."

PARACELSUS

"Our larger tricks, and our daily provisions, and all the other things we want, we get out of that hat . . . And you know, sir, if you'll excuse me saying it, there isn't a wholesale shop, not for Genuine Magic goods sir. I don't know if you noticed our inscription—the Genuine Magic Shop. . . . There is absolutely no deception, sir."

H.G. WELLS

All the Powers of the world, the heavens and the star peoples, and the red and blue sacred days; all things that move in the universe, in the rivers the brooks, the springs,k all waters, all trees that stand, all the grasses of our Grandmother, all the sacred peoples of the universe: Listen!

BLACK ELK

I've a green charm for woods,
And a blue charm for water,
And a silver for moons
When they're in the first quarter.

I've a slow charm for growth,
And a swift one for birds,
And a soft one for sleep,
And a sweet one for words,

I've a long charm for love,
And a strong charm for youth,
And one you can't change
Or destroy, for the truth.

ELEANOR FARJEON

Magicians and the practice of magic have been relegated to myth, folklore, and tales for children, and as such are just stories.

ELIZABETH RATISSEAU

A fine story—whether for children of adults—should reflect both dark and light, both shadow and glare. Look back into folklore and legend, myth and religion , and you will find much of the emphasis is on the shadow. A shadowless man is a monster, a devil, a thing of evil . A man without a shadow is soulless. A shadow without a man is a pitiable shred. Yet together, light and dark, they make a whole. And these light/dark chiaroscuro figures, walking about a magical landscape illumine all our lives.

JANE YOLEN

Whatever spirits have come together here, either belonging to the earth or living in the air, let all spirits be happy, and then listen attentively to what is said. Therefore, O spirits, do ye all pay attention, show kindness to the human race who both day and night bring their offerings; therefore protect them strenuously.

PALI LITERATURE

His fingertip may change
The shapes we live within
To forms with spirits strange
And creatures queer of skin.

ELEANOR FARJEON

If we do not find miracles, we create them,
and , since most of us learned something
about the world, for better or worse, from fairy
tales, from myth and legend, we sometimes
say: "Four, yes, of course; but once in a while—
why not?—five or three."

MARJORIE FISCHER

Make your choice, come and change.

Which will you be,

Which creature of earth or air,

Sky and sea?

Scale and fin, fur and hair,

All are waiting still;

Come with unfaltering feet,

For change is sure and sweet

Into anything you dare,

Anything you will

HERBERT ASQUITH

The forces of nature can be regarded as supernatural agencies distinct from others, such as gods, ancestors, ghosts, and other conceptions of spiritual beings. Most things in nature are motivated by forces which are programmed for specific action, usually in systemic interdependence with other forces. If left alone they will act as programmed, independent of human or spiritual instigation. . . .The concepts of mana and its presumed parallels (e.g., Iroquois orenda, Algonquian manitou, Sioux wakan, Malay kramat, Indian brahma, Greek dynamis), which were noted by early scholars . . . are specific cultural variations on a concept of a mystical power that seems universal. Such power is in all things, natural and supernatural.

PHILLIPS STEVENS JR

The ancient adepts or Magi had taught the essential truths of all the great religions of the world. They taught that the physical world and the mental world existed in the continuum of one great mind, the eternal reconciler of all opposites, the source of all things at all levels, the ultimate and the absolute repository of wisdom and knowledge. Man with his limited intelligence could never comprehend the incomprehensible. But knowledge of God was accessible to man through his perception of truth and spiritual values . . . The ancient belief was summed up in the formula carved on ruined temples: "I am all that is, all that was, all that will be, and no one shall lift my veil."

WADE BASKIN

MAGICIANS & ENCHANTERS

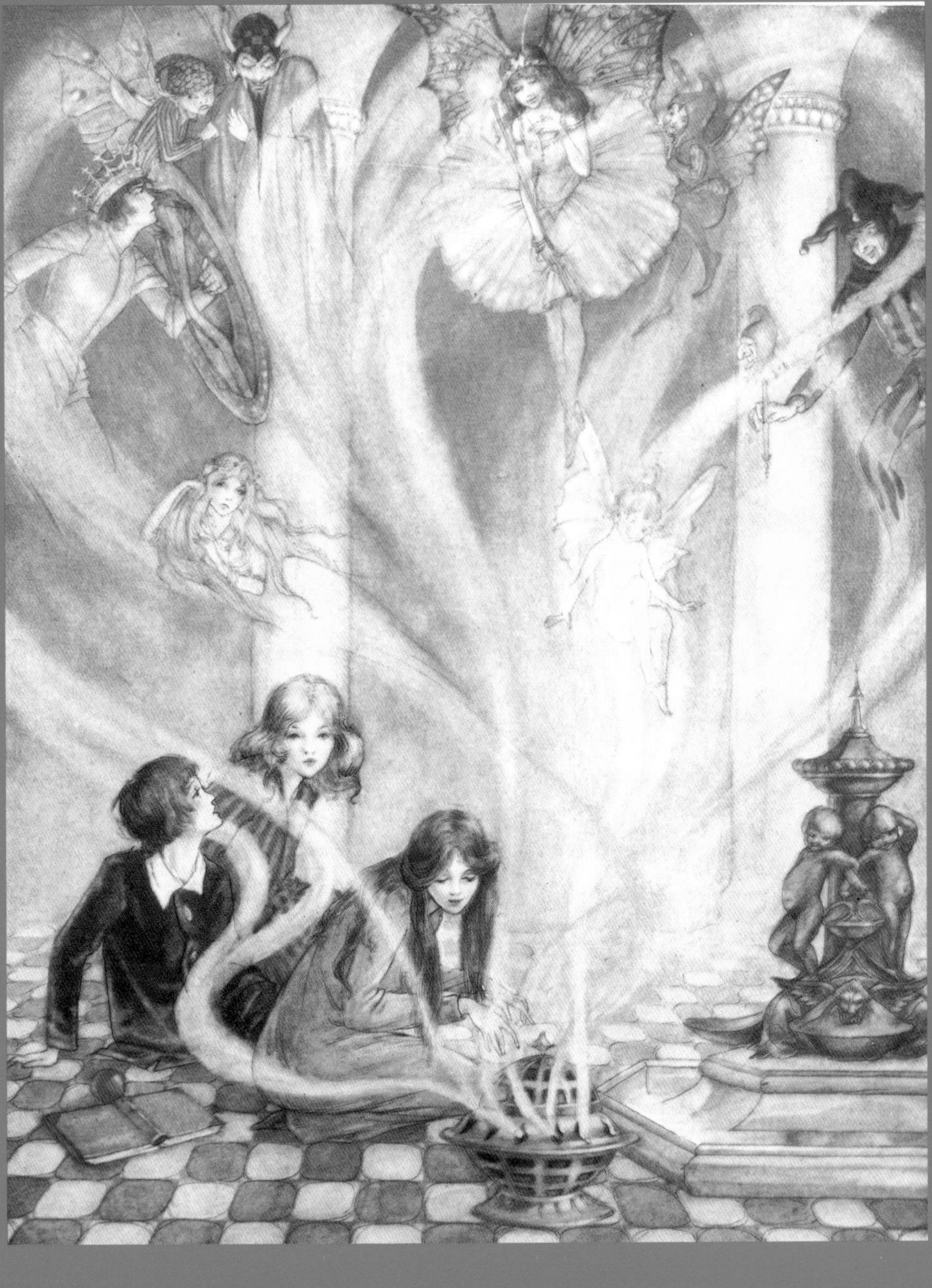

Now I want

Spirits to enforce, art to enchant;

And my ending is despair

Unless I be relieved by prayer,

Which pierces so that it assaults

Mercy itself and frees all faults

SHAKESPEARE

Magic is the traditional science of the secrets of Nature which has been trans-muted to us from the Magi. By means of this science the adept is invested with a species of relative omnipotence and can operate superhumanly—that is, after a manner which transcends the normal possibility of men.

ELIPHAS LEVI

There goes neither the eye, nor speech,
nor the mind: we know It not; nor do we
see how to teach one about It. Different
It is from all that are known, and It is
beyond the unknown as well.

KENA UPANISHAD 1.3

*We behold, then, by the sight of the mind, in
that eternal truth from which all things tem-
poral are made, the form according to which
we are, and according to which we do anything by true and right reason, either in our-
selves, or in things corporeal; and we have the
true knowledge of things, thence conceived, as
it were as a word within us, and by speaking
we beget it from within; nor by being born does
it depart from us.*

ST. AUGUSTINE

The habits of a lifetime and basic structure of nearly all our thought impel us so strong-
ly into dismissing supernaturalism as such, that it requires constant and sometimes
strenuous effort to break away from this negative credulity, although it is as blindly
prejudicial as the most naïve superstitions about ghosts and fortune-tellers. Most of us
carelessly define "spirit" and supernature as entities or functions that are not physical,
intellectual, or emotional.

MARY MCDERMOTT SHIDELER

MAGICIANS & ENCHANTERS

PICTURE CREDITS

Cover	John William Waterhouse. "The Magic Circle," 1886.
Endpapers.	Maxfield Parrish. "The Pied Piper," 1909.
Half Title	John William Waterhouse. "Circe Invidiosa," 1892.
Frontis	Karel Viteslav Masek. "The Prophetess Libuse," c. 1893.
Title	Margaret Tarrant. From *An Alphabet of Magic*, 1928.
Copyright	Julius Schnorr. "Moses Informs Pharaoh of the Will of Jehovah," n.d.
2	Unknown. Babylonian depiction of Gilgamesh.
3	Unknown. "Papyrus of Nespakashuty," c. 1000 BC
4	Monro S. Orr. From *Stories from the Arabian Nights,* 1913.
5	Virginia Sterrett. From *Old French Fairy Tales*, 1920.
6	Edmund Dulac. "Open Sesame!," c. 1910.
7	Warwick Goble. From *Folktales of Bengal*, 1912.
8	John William Waterhouse. "Circe Offering the Cup to Ulysses," 1891.
9	Frederick Sandys. "Medea," 1866.
11	J.A. Knapp. From *An Encyclopedia of Masonic, Hermetic, Qabbalistic and Rosicrucian Symbolical Philosophy*, 1928.
13	N.C. Wyeth. From *The Boy's King Arthur*, 1917.
14	Charles Folkard. From *The Arabian Nights*, 1913.
15	N.C. Wyeth. From *The Mysterious Stranger*, 1916.
16	H. Artelius. From *Hinter den Blauen Bergen*, c. 1910.
17	Alexander Evariste Fragonard. "The Magician," n.d.

18   Piero della Vecchia. "The Chiromant," (detail) 17th century.

19   Piero della Vecchia. "The Chiromant," 17th century.

20   Edmund Dulac. "Father Time," c. 1910.

21   Konstantin Somov. "Sorcery," c. 1898.

22   W.H. Walker. "More Than He Expected," c. 1910.

23   W.H. Margetson. From *Stories From Grimm*, c. 1900

24   Ruth Cobb. From *Wonder Voyage*, c. 1910.

25   Walter Zweigle. From *Es War Einmal*, n.d.

26   Warwick Goble. From *Stories from the Pentamerone*, 1911.

27   A.H. Watson. From *Princess Elizabeth's Gift Book*, c. 1930.

28   W.H. Margetson. From *Stories From Grimm*, c. 1900

29   Florence M. Anderson. From *Blackie's Children's Annual*, c. 1920.

30   Edward Burne-Jones. "Sibylla Delphica," 1868.

31   Unknown. From *The World's Best Fairy Stories*, 1911.

32   Harry Watrous. "The Magician," 1914.

33   Frederick Leighton. "The Star of Bethlehem," 1862.

Back Cover   Dugald Stewart Walker. From *The Boy Apprenticed to an Enchanter*, 1920.

                    R. Savage. From *Queen Mab's Fairy Realm*, 1901.